j363.348 Kalman, Bobbie,
KAL   1947-

         Emergency workers are
         on their way!

$22.60

DATE			

EMERGENCY WORKERS
are on their way!

Bobbie Kalman

Crabtree Publishing Company

www.crabtreebooks.com

Created by Bobbie Kalman

Dedicated by Lisa Maisonneuve
To Colin, the finest cop in our household and Eliana, our little miracle

Author and Editor-in-Chief
Bobbie Kalman

Substantive editor
Kathryn Smithyman

Project editor and research
Reagan Miller

Editors
Molly Aloian
Kristina Lundblad
Kelley MacAulay

Art director
Robert MacGregor

Design
Margaret Amy Reiach
Samantha Crabtree (series logo)

Production coordinator
Katherine Kantor

Photo research
Crystal Foxton

Consultant
Holly Harington, FEMA Office of Public Affairs,
U.S. Department of Homeland Security

Special thanks to
FEMA, Warren L. Maye and The Salvation Army,
and Warren Faidley from Weatherstock

Photographs
AP/Wide World Photos: pages 21, 27 (bottom), 29
Marc Crabtree: pages 18, 30, 31
©FEMA: pages 9 (top), 14 (top), 26
Photo by Warren L. Maye, The Salvation Army:
    page 27 (top)
Romeo/V&W/Seapics.com: page 19
©Weatherstock/Warren Faidley: pages 22, 23 (bottom)
Image by John Wehr: page 25
Other images by Brand X Pictures, Digital Stock,
Digital Vision, Image Source, and Photodisc

Illustrations
Barbara Bedell: page 8
Margaret Amy Reiach: page 29

Crabtree Publishing Company
www.crabtreebooks.com   1-800-387-7650

Cataloging-in-Publication Data
Kalman, Bobbie.
    Emergency workers are on their way! / Bobbie Kalman.
      p. cm. -- (My community and its helpers series)
    Includes index.
    ISBN 0-7787-2094-2 (RLB) -- ISBN 0-7787-2122-1 (pbk.)
    1. Police--Juvenile literature. 2. Fire fighters--Juvenile literature.
3. Emergency medical technicians--Juvenile literature. 4. Rescue
work--Juvenile literature. 5. Disaster relief--Juvenile literature.
I. Title.
    HV7922.K36 2005
    363.34'81--dc22
                                                2004014157
                                                LC

**Published in
the United States**
PMB16A
350 Fifth Ave.
Suite 3308
New York, NY
10118

**Published
in Canada**
616 Welland Ave.,
St. Catharines, Ontario
Canada
L2M 5V6

**Published in the
United Kingdom**
73 Lime Walk
Headington
Oxford
OX3 7AD
United Kingdom

**Published
in Australia**
386 Mt. Alexander Rd.,
Ascot Vale (Melbourne)
VIC 3032

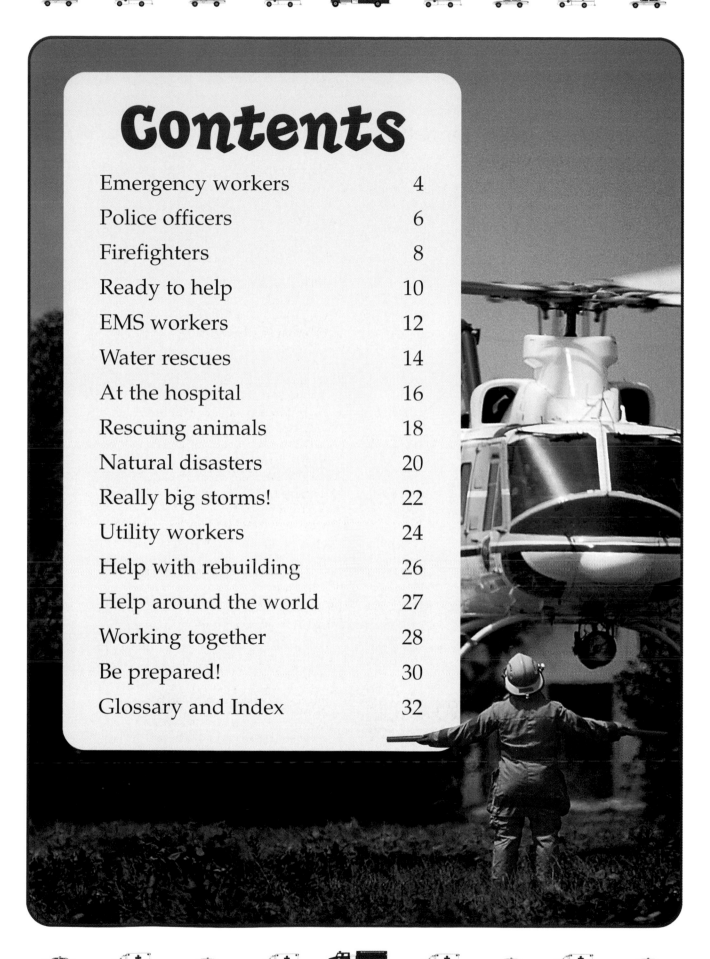

Contents

Emergency workers   4

Police officers   6

Firefighters   8

Ready to help   10

EMS workers   12

Water rescues   14

At the hospital   16

Rescuing animals   18

Natural disasters   20

Really big storms!   22

Utility workers   24

Help with rebuilding   26

Help around the world   27

Working together   28

Be prepared!   30

Glossary and Index   32

Emergency workers

Rescue workers search for people who are missing and *rescue*, or save, them. They often use dogs to help them find people.

Emergency workers are people who are trained to help others during **emergencies**. Emergencies are serious situations that happen suddenly. People usually do not expect emergencies and may not be ready for them. Emergency workers are always prepared to act quickly when emergencies happen.

Types of emergencies

There are many types of emergencies. Accidents, fires, floods, earthquakes, and explosions are all emergencies. During emergencies, people are often hurt, and their homes and belongings may be destroyed. Emergencies can be scary, but emergency workers know how to help!

What are community helpers?

Emergency workers are **community helpers**.
A **community** is an area and the people who
live in that area. Community helpers are people
who help keep communities safe and healthy.
Police officers, firefighters, construction workers,
and teachers are other community helpers.

Police officers

Police officers make sure that people obey the laws in their communities. They are often the first emergency workers at an emergency. After a car accident, for example, police officers clear the roads so other emergency workers can get through. Some police officers are trained to give **first aid** to **injured**, or hurt, people. First aid is medical help. Police officers are also trained to search for people who are missing or lost.

*Some police officers **patrol** communities to keep them safe.*

Lights and sirens

Most police officers drive cars with flashing lights and sirens. The bright lights and loud sirens let people know that the police are on their way. Some police officers ride bicycles or drive motorcycles instead of cars. Both are smaller than cars and can go places where cars cannot go. Bicycles and motorcycles ride easily over rough dirt trails.

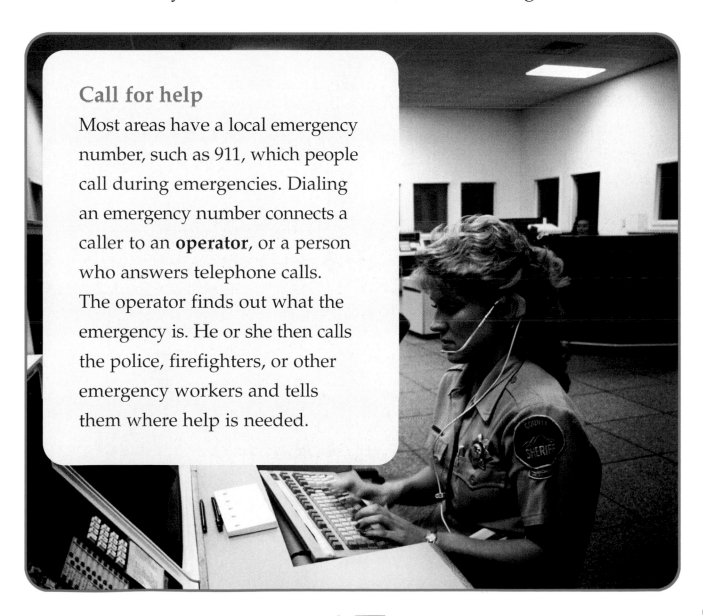

Call for help

Most areas have a local emergency number, such as 911, which people call during emergencies. Dialing an emergency number connects a caller to an **operator**, or a person who answers telephone calls. The operator finds out what the emergency is. He or she then calls the police, firefighters, or other emergency workers and tells them where help is needed.

Firefighters

Firefighters help at many kinds of emergencies. Their main jobs are to put out fires and to rescue people. To perform these jobs, firefighters use different kinds of tools and equipment.

They use long hoses to spray water onto flames. They use axes to break open doors and windows. Firefighters climb tall ladders to reach people who are trapped high up in burning buildings.

Fighting wildfires

Firefighters fight **wildfires** as well. Wildfires are fires in forests and parklands. Hundreds or even thousands of firefighters work together to put out these fires. They fight wildfires from the ground and from the air.

Some firefighters fly airplanes and helicopters that have large tanks for holding water or other liquids. The liquids are dropped onto wildfires.

These firefighters are working together to stop a wildfire from spreading. Some large fires take several days or even weeks to put out.

Ready to help

Firefighters are also trained to help in other emergencies, such as car accidents. They rush to accidents to free people who are trapped in cars. They use tools, such as large saws, to reach and rescue people who are trapped. Firefighters also help when there are floods, earthquakes, and explosions.

All firefighters are trained to give first aid to injured people. Some firefighters are specially trained to help people with more serious injuries, such as burns or broken bones. They **examine**, or carefully check, people who are hurt. The firefighters care for injured people until ambulances arrive.

*These firefighters are using a **stretcher** to move an injured person to an ambulance.*
A stretcher is a cloth- or plastic-covered frame that is used to move people who have been hurt.

*Firefighters help land **medevacs**, or helicopters in which people are flown to hospitals.*

EMS workers

Emergency medical service, or "EMS" workers are people who are trained to give medical care to sick or injured people. **Paramedics** are EMS workers with additional medical training. Paramedics can give people medicines and are trained to use different kinds of medical equipment. EMS workers drive sick or injured people to hospitals in ambulances. Ambulances contain medical supplies such as bandages, medicines, and **oxygen tanks**. EMS workers use these medical supplies to **stabilize** people. To stabilize means to keep a person's illnesses or injuries from getting worse. EMS workers move people into ambulances on **gurneys**, as shown below. They then drive injured people to hospitals, where doctors and nurses give them medical care.

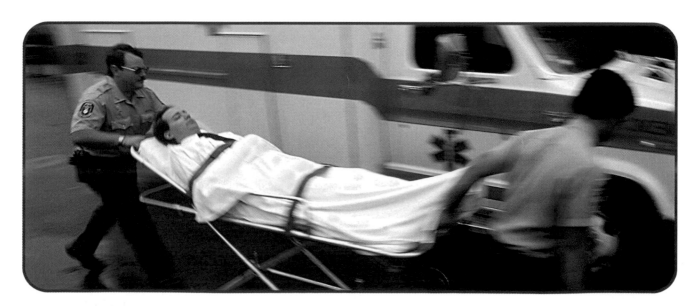

It is important that ambulances arrive at emergencies quickly. Their loud sirens and flashing lights warn other drivers to get off the road and let the ambulances through.

Medevacs

Some EMS workers also fly helicopters called medevacs. Medevacs are often used to reach injured people in places that are far from major roads. They have medical supplies and equipment on board. EMS workers use these supplies to give people first aid while the helicopters are flying. Medevacs are also used to **transport**, or move, **patients** from one hospital to another. Patients may need to be moved to special hospitals, such as children's hospitals or hospitals that treat serious burns.

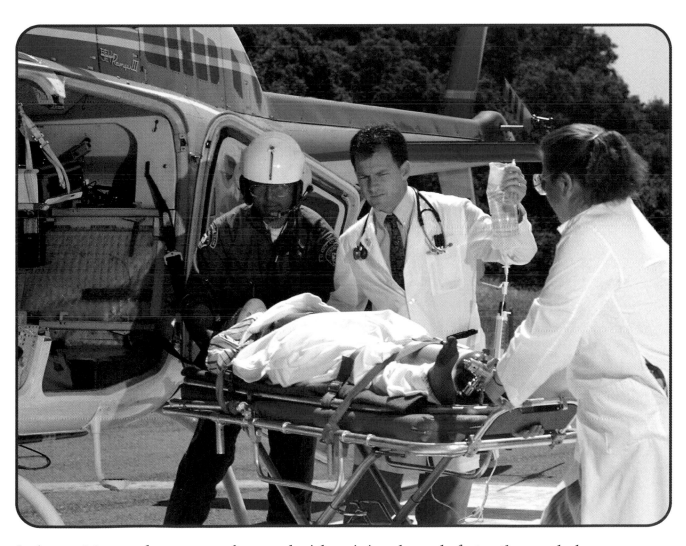

In large cities, medevacs can often reach sick or injured people faster than ambulances can. Ambulances are often slowed down by traffic on busy roads and freeways.

Water rescues

Specially trained police officers, firefighters, and EMS workers rescue people whose boats are caught in dangerous storms.

***Lifeguards** are trained to rescue drowning swimmers. Lifeguards at public beaches often watch swimmers from **lifeguard towers**, as shown above.*

Emergencies can happen when people swim or go boating in rivers, lakes, and oceans. Communities that are near water usually have police officers, firefighters, and EMS workers who are trained to rescue people in water.

Water-rescue equipment

Emergency workers use special equipment during water rescues. They use rescue boats with loud sirens and bright lights to rescue people on small boats that have drifted too far from shore. The rescue boats are stocked with medical supplies that can be used to help people who are injured on the drifting boats. People who have fallen through thin ice on frozen lakes or rivers also need help. Firefighters use ropes, **harnesses**, and other equipment to pull these people from the icy waters.

The Coast Guard

National **Coast Guards** patrol oceans in large boats. There are many **crews**, or groups, of Coast Guard workers. One group, called the **search-and-rescue crew**, is made up of emergency workers.

From the air

Members of the search-and-rescue crew sometimes help other emergency workers rescue people from boats that are lost in the ocean. They also rescue people from boats that have **capsized**, or turned over. The search-and-rescue crew sometimes uses helicopters to pull people out of the water. Helicopters can often reach people who need help faster than boats can reach them.

During a helicopter rescue, a member of the search-and-rescue crew, called a **winchman***, is lowered down to the water on a* **cable***, or wire. He or she then grabs the person in need of help and pulls him or her into the helicopter.*

Doctors and nurses are ready to care for sick or injured people as soon as EMS workers arrive at a hospital. Some doctors and nurses work in the **emergency room** or "ER." The ER is the part of a hospital in which emergency medical care is given. EMS workers use radios or cell phones to call ahead to tell the ER doctors about the patients' illnesses or injuries. The doctors and nurses can then prepare for the patients. Doctors and nurses work quickly to treat many patients at the same time. The patients have different sicknesses or injuries, including broken bones, deep cuts, and burns.

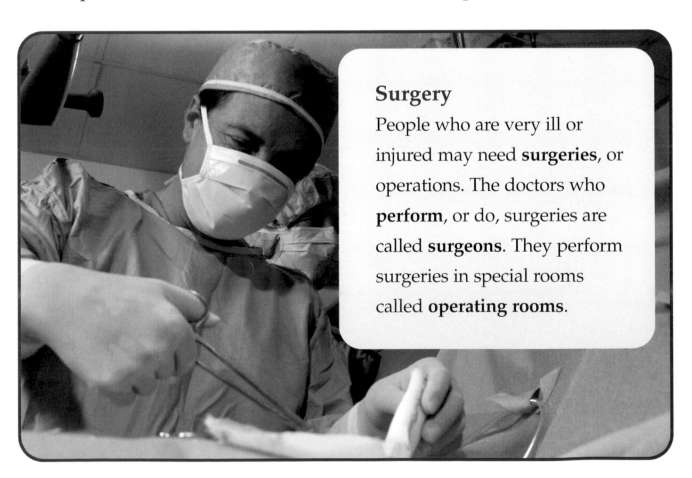

Surgery
People who are very ill or injured may need **surgeries**, or operations. The doctors who **perform**, or do, surgeries are called **surgeons**. They perform surgeries in special rooms called **operating rooms**.

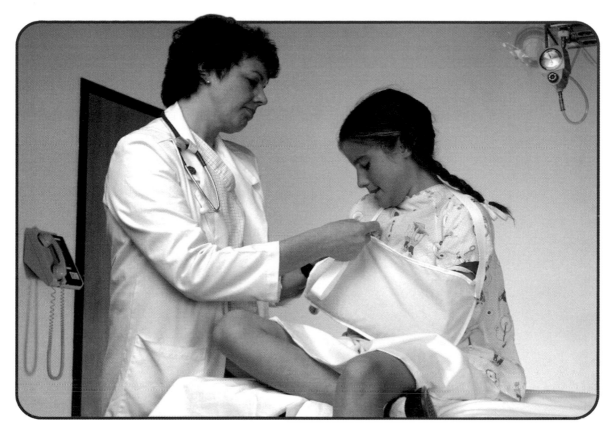

Jennifer's emergency

Jennifer fell off her bicycle and hurt her arm. Her parents quickly drove her to the ER. At first, Jennifer was scared of going to the hospital, but she stopped feeling frightened as soon as she met Dr. Campbell. Dr. Campbell was very kind and told Jennifer not to be afraid. She took an **x-ray** of Jennifer's arm. By looking at the x-ray, Dr. Campbell discovered that Jennifer's arm was broken.

Dr. Campbell put Jennifer's arm into a **cast**. She explained that the cast would protect the broken bone and keep it still so the bone could heal. Once the cast was on, the doctor put a **sling** around Jennifer's arm to support it. Dr. Campbell told Jennifer that her friends could sign her cast with colorful markers or decorate it with stickers. Jennifer thanked Dr. Campbell for taking such good care of her!

Rescuing animals

Animals have emergencies, too, so there are emergency workers to help them. If a dog gets hit by a car, for example, it may need to be taken to a **veterinarian**. Veterinarians or "vets" are doctors who care for animals. A vet will treat the dog's injuries and make sure the animal heals properly. Vets also perform surgeries on animals with serious injuries or illnesses.

Animal shelters
Animal shelters are places where people care for lost animals. They also take in animals that are treated badly by their owners. Animal-shelter workers rescue animals that are in trouble and look after them.

This animal-shelter vet is caring for a lost dog. Most of the animals at shelters are frightened, so he is gentle with the dog.

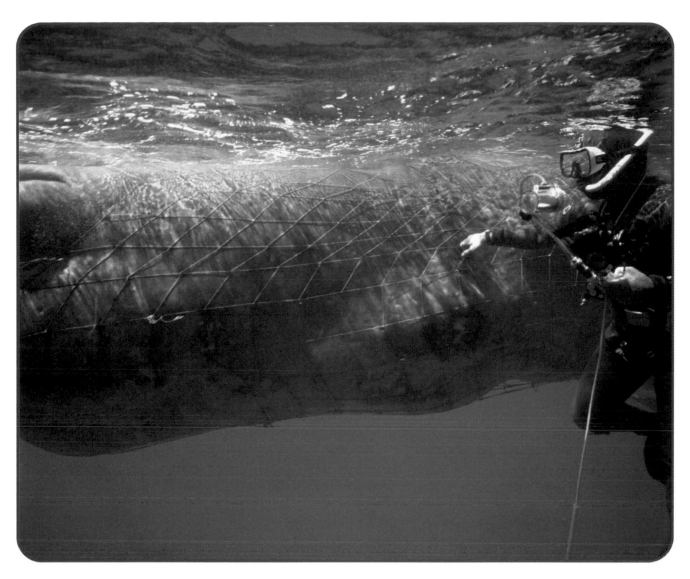

To the rescue!

Wildlife rescue workers are people who are trained to rescue **wild**, or untamed, animals from danger. For example, whales sometimes get tangled in fishing nets. A whale that is caught in a fishing net may die if it cannot swim to the surface of the water to breathe.

To free the whale from a fishing net, a wildlife rescue worker cuts away the net around the whale's body, as shown above. Before the wildlife rescue worker returns to the surface, he will make sure the whale has not been injured by the net.

Natural disasters

Natural disasters are emergencies caused by nature. Floods and earthquakes are two types of natural disasters that damage homes and other buildings, trees, roads, and vehicles. Hundreds or even thousands of emergency workers are needed to help people during these terrible disasters.

Floods

Floods occur when too much rain falls in an area or when too much snow melts at one time. The extra water fills rivers and lakes, causing them to overflow into towns and cities. Flood waters sometimes rush so fast that they carry away cars and even houses! Firefighters, police officers, and other emergency workers use helicopters and boats to save people and animals from flood waters. Emergency workers also fill large plastic bags with sand. They stack the sand bags on top of one another along the banks of rivers to make **barriers**, or walls. The barriers help hold the flood waters away from roads and homes.

Earthquakes

Earthquakes are natural disasters that occur when the ground shakes with great force. Although earthquakes last only a few moments, they are very dangerous! Earthquakes can cause buildings, bridges, and highways to **collapse**, or fall to the ground. Emergency workers have to act quickly to find people who are trapped inside the cars or buildings. Rescue workers dig through **rubble**, or broken building materials, to find people who may be trapped underneath.

Firefighters, police officers, and other emergency workers carefully dig through collapsed buildings, making sure that more rubble does not fall on the people trapped underneath.

Really big storms!

Blizzards, tornadoes, and hurricanes are other types of natural disasters. When these emergencies happen, many types of emergency workers are called to help. Firefighters, police officers, EMS workers, and snow-removal crews all help rescue people.

Blizzards

Blizzards are snowstorms with strong winds. When people drive during a blizzard, they cannot see very far ahead of their cars. Many people skid off slippery roads or become trapped in their cars.

During blizzards, strong winds and blowing snow make it difficult for emergency workers to reach the people who need help. Emergency workers often use snowmobiles to reach people who are stranded.

Whirling winds

Tornadoes and hurricanes are powerful storms that destroy homes, cars, and boats. The winds are so strong that they can toss large objects such as trees, mailboxes, and even cars into the air! Hurricane winds also carry a lot of rain, causing areas to flood.

A tornado, shown above, is a moving column of wind that reaches down to the ground.

After the fact

After a tornado or a hurricane, emergency workers and volunteers look for people who are trapped inside buildings. Emergency workers often have to dig through rubble to find them. Many **power lines** are knocked down by these huge storms, leaving people without electricity. **Utility workers** are people who repair the power lines.

Emergency workers help clean up the many objects that have been scattered by strong hurricane winds.

utility workers

These utility workers are wearing special boots, hardhats, and safety harnesses while they work on power lines high above the ground.

Utilities are community services such as electricity, running water, and telephone service. These services are provided to buildings in a community through equipment such as power lines, water pipes, and telephone lines. During natural disasters, this equipment is often damaged, causing problems such as **power outages**, or loss of electrical power to a community.

Different jobs

Utility workers are people who repair utility equipment. Different utility workers repair different equipment. Power lines are repaired by **electricians**. **Plumbers** fix damaged water pipes. Telephone lines are repaired by telephone-company workers. These emergency workers make sure that people have the utilities they need in their communities.

No power!

Power outages often happen without warning. During a power outage, trains, subways, elevators, and traffic lights all suddenly shut down. Utility workers must work quickly to fix the problems and restore power to a community. When a power outage occurs, firefighters rush to rescue people who may be trapped in elevators or subways. Police officers help direct traffic because the traffic lights do not work. Police officers also have to make sure that people do not break into shops and **loot**, or steal. Hospital emergency rooms are very busy during power outages because people often get hurt.

Help with rebuilding

Natural disasters and other emergencies cause a lot of damage to communities. Homes, schools, and other buildings often need major repairs. Some buildings need to be rebuilt completely! Large organizations, such as the the U.S. Department of Homeland Security's **Federal Emergency Management Agency** or "FEMA," help communities recover from disasters.

FEMA workers help people make repairs to their homes or find safe places to live when their homes have been badly damaged or destroyed. They teach people how to prepare for emergencies and how to make their homes safer. FEMA workers also show communities how to build safer, stronger buildings that will not be easily damaged by natural disasters.

Help around the world

After a natural disaster, thousands of people in a country may need help to survive. Organizations such as the **Salvation Army** and the **Red Cross and Red Crescent Societies** travel all over the world to help people. They provide people who have been affected by natural disasters with food and medical care.

These Salvation Army workers are wearing masks to prevent them from breathing in the dust of collapsed buildings.

Famine and war

The Red Cross and Red Crescent Society workers also assist communities during times of **famine** and war. A famine is a long period of time during which people have no food. The workers give people food and teach them how to grow food crops. During times of war, the workers care for injured and sick people.

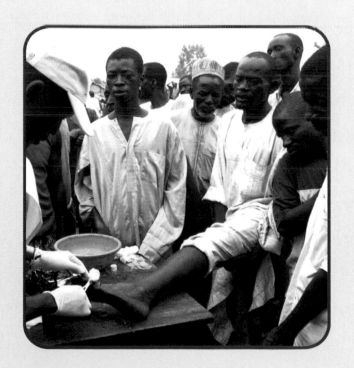

Working together

When an emergency happens, all the people in a community must work together. People who are not emergency workers may be asked to help clean up and repair damaged property. For example, after earthquakes or tornadoes, construction workers help by using equipment such as bulldozers and cranes to remove rubble from collapsed buildings. Plumbers and other utility workers repair broken pipes and fix the water and gas lines in a community. Many people **volunteer** to clean up the streets near their homes.

Ways to help

After an emergency, many jobs need to be done. If you want to volunteer in your community after an emergency, contact your local volunteer organizations to find out the best ways you can help. Listed below are a few suggestions for ways you could lend a hand to help others during and after an emergency. You can make a difference!

- Check on your neighbors to make sure they are safe. Share your food and water with people who do not have enough.

- Remove branches, garbage, and other objects from your property and from your neighborhood.

- Help emergency workers hand out food, water, clothing, and blankets to people who need them. You can also help feed the emergency workers who are working in your community!

Be prepared!

Emergencies can happen without warning, so it is important to be prepared at all times. Here are some important safety tips that will help you and your family prepare for an emergency.

A firefighter or your local fire chief will answer any questions you may have about fire safety.

Making a plan

It is important for every family to have a **family disaster plan**. A family disaster plan is a set of rules that everyone in your home should follow during an emergency. The plan needs to include a meeting place outside your home where everyone will gather once they are safely out of the home.

For example, you and your family may agree to meet at a neighbor's house if a fire breaks out. Choose a relative or a family friend to call if you become separated from your family during an emergency. By calling this person, you can let your family know where you are.

Staying safe

Being prepared will help you and your family stay calm during an emergency. Listed below are a few simple ways you and your family can prepare for emergencies.

- Be sure your home has a working smoke alarm. Change the batteries twice a year.

- Always make sure your pets wear collars with identification tags. If a pet gets lost during an emergency, the tags will let people know where to find you so they can return your pet to you.

- Make a **disaster supply kit**. The kit will help you and your family during a natural disaster. It should have bottles of water, canned foods, warm clothing, flashlights, and medical supplies. A radio that runs on batteries will also be useful if your community loses electricity. Don't forget to include extra batteries!

Glossary

Note: Boldfaced words that are defined in the text may not appear in the glossary.

cast A hard covering that is used to keep an injured body part from moving

gurney A narrow bed on wheels that is used to move patients

harness A strong strap or band used to hold and control a person or an animal

oxygen tank A tank containing oxygen that is used to help people breathe more easily

patient A person who is receiving medical care

patrol To move around an area and guard it to make sure people are safe

power lines Long wires that carry electricity

sling A piece of cloth that is looped around a person's neck to support an injured arm

volunteer To offer to help without being asked or paid

x-ray A photograph of the inside of a person's body

Index

animal shelters 18
blizzards 22
Coast Guard 15
doctors 12, 16-17, 18
earthquakes 4, 10, 20, 21, 28
EMS workers 12-13, 14, 16, 22

firefighters 5, 7, 8-11, 14, 20, 21, 22, 25, 30
first aid 6, 10, 13
flood 4, 10, 20, 23
hurricanes 22, 23
nurses 16
police officers 5, 6-7, 14, 20, 21, 22, 25

Red Cross 27
Salvation Army 27
tornadoes 22, 23, 28
utility workers 23, 24-25, 28
veterinarians 18
volunteers 28, 29
wildlife rescue workers 19

1 2 3 4 5 6 7 8 9 0   Printed in the U.S.A.   4 3 2 1 0 9 8 7 6 5

8456

EASE SHAI